My Favorite Dogs

BEAGLE

Jinny Johnson

A⁺

Smart Apple Media

Published by Smart Apple Media
P.O. Box 1329
Mankato, MN 56002

Printed in the United States of America,
at Corporate Graphics in North Mankato, Minnesota.

Designed by Hel James
Edited by Mary-Jane Wilkins

Library of Congress Cataloging-in-Publication Data

Johnson, Jinny, 1949-
Beagle / by Jinny Johnson.
    p. cm. -- (My favorite dogs)
Includes index.
ISBN 978-1-59920-839-8 (hardcover, library bound)
1. Beagle (Dog breed)--Juvenile literature. I. Title.
SF429.B3J64 2013
636.753'7--dc23
                    2012008596

Photo acknowledgements
l = left, r = right; t = top, b = bottom
page 1 Miroslav K/Shutterstock; 3 Eric Isselée/Shutterstock;
4-5 verityjohnson/Shutterstock; 6 Glen Jones/Shutterstock;
7 iStockphoto/Thinkstock; 8-9 Hemera/Thinkstock; 10 terekhov igor/Shutterstock;
11 teekaygee/Shutterstock; 12t Eric Isselée/Shutterstock, b AnetaPics/Shutterstock;
13t AnetaPics/Shutterstock, b Eric Isselée/Shutterstock; 14-15 Gnilenkov Aleksey/
Shutterstock; 16 Pukhov Konstantin/Shutterstock; 17 Northsweden/Shutterstock;
18 Hemera/Thinkstock; 19 ARENA Creative; 20 Monika Wisniewska/Shutterstock;
21 Hemera/Thinkstock; 22 Monika Wisniewska/Shutterstock;
23 Neftali/Shutterstock.com
Cover Eric Isselée/Shutterstock

DAD0504c
072013
9 8 7 6 5 4 3

Contents

I'm a Beagle!

I'm friendly and fun, and people say I'm a great family dog.

I'm not too big, I'm easy to look after, and I love other pets and children!

5

What I Need

I've got lots of energy and I like a good long walk every day. I like lots of company too, so don't leave me alone for too long.

I like to roll around in stuff that smells good to me, but I'm happy to have a bath when you think I need one.

The Beagle

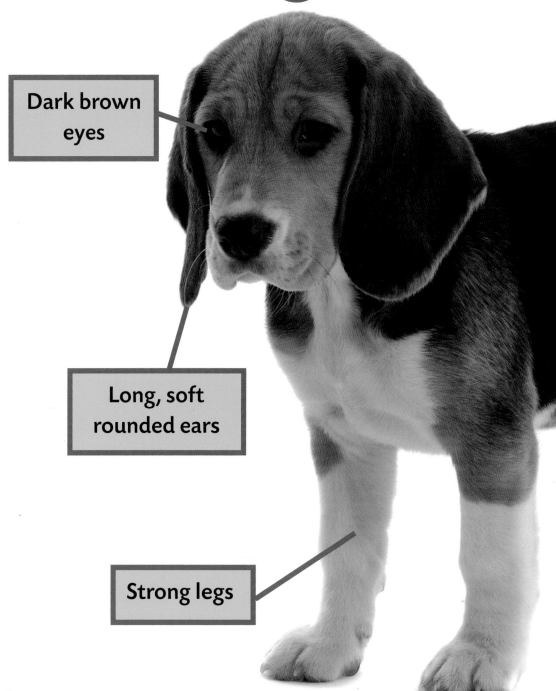

Dark brown eyes

Long, soft rounded ears

Strong legs

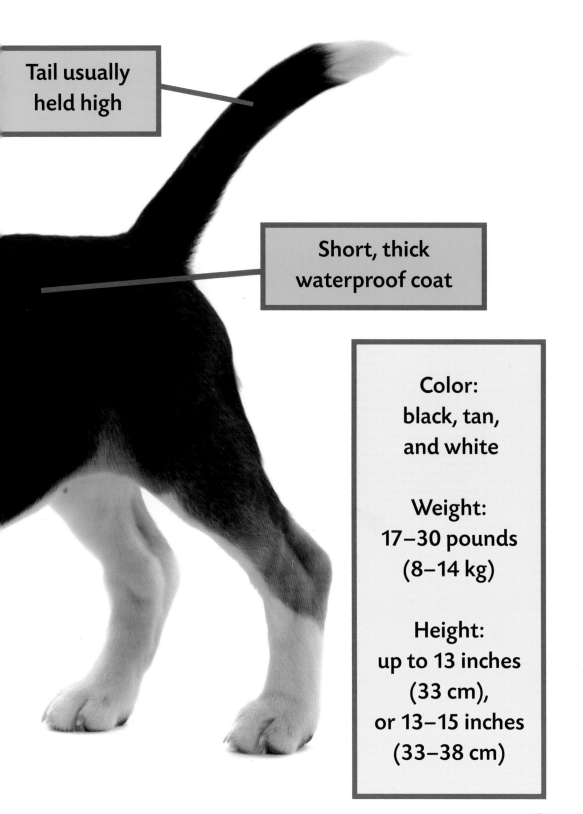

Tail usually held high

Short, thick waterproof coat

Color: black, tan, and white

Weight: 17–30 pounds (8–14 kg)

Height: up to 13 inches (33 cm), or 13–15 inches (33–38 cm)

All About Beagles

Beagles are a popular dog breed today, and they have been around for hundreds of years. They have always been used as hunting dogs.

Beagles also enjoy taking part in agility competitions. The dogs have to run and jump round special courses with different obstacles.

Growing Up

So cute! A four-week-old beagle looks adorable, but he needs to stay with his mom.

At eight weeks, a beagle pup is ready for a new home.

A three-
month-old
beagle pup
is a bundle
of fun.

At five months,
a beagle is
growing up fast.

Follow the Nose

Beagles have an amazing sense of smell and they love to follow an interesting scent.

A beagle's sense of smell is 40 times as powerful as a human's.

Specially trained beagles work at airports to sniff out forbidden foods in passengers' luggage.

Training Your Beagle

Beagles are smart dogs and they are quick to learn. Start training your puppy when he is young. Be patient and kind and never shout at your dog.

Beagles don't bark a lot,
but they do bark loudly.

Beagles love food
rewards, but they
are greedy, so don't
give your puppy too
many treats.

Watch Out!

Smell is everything to a beagle. If he smells something good he will follow it—and forget about you and his training.

Make sure your beagle can't get out of your garden or yard by himself.

Your Healthy Beagle

Beagles are healthy dogs and have few problems. Take your pet to the vet regularly to make sure he is fit and well.

Brush your beagle's coat a few times a week. Watch out for those long ears and keep them clean.

Beagles love to roll in smelly things so will sometimes need a bath.

Caring for Your Beagle

You and your family must think very carefully before buying a dog. Dogs live for many years and need lots of attention. Every day your

dog will need food, water, and exercise, as well as love and care. It will also need to be taken to the vet for vaccinations.

One of the most famous beagles of all is Snoopy. He is the pet of Charlie Brown in the 'Peanuts' cartoon strip.

Useful Words

agility competitions
Events where dogs run around
courses with obstacles and jumps.

breed
A particular type of dog.

vaccinations
Injections given by the vet to protect
your dog against certain illnesses.

Index